JB JOSSEY-BASS™
A Wiley Brand

Memorial & In-tribute Gifts

49 Ideas for Increasing Memorial and In-tribute Gift Support

Scott C. Stevenson, Editor

WILEY

Memorial and In-tribute Gifts
51 Ideas for Increasing
Memorial & In-tribute Gift Support

Published by

Stevenson, Inc.

P.O. Box 4528 • Sioux City, Iowa • 51104
Phone 712.239.3010 • Fax 712.239.2166

www.stevensoninc.com

51 Ideas for Increasing Memorial & In-tribute Gift Support

Table of Contents

51 Ideas for Increasing Memorial & In-tribute Gift Support

Table of Contents

Memorial, In-tribute Giving

51 Ideas for Increasing Memorial & In-tribute Gift Support

1 Point Out Recent Memorials and Their Uses

Memorial gifts help honor the memory of loved ones and friends, they build loyalty to the recipient charity and they can help broaden a charity's base of support.

If your organization deserves to be the recipient of more memorial gifts, show the public how much you treasure them:

✓ Include a list of all memorials (and those who gave to them) in your annual honor roll of contributors.

✓ Mention recent memorials in each issue of the newsletter or magazine you distribute to your mailing list.

✓ Personally thank everyone who makes a memorial contribution and inform the family of those who contributed and how much.

✓ Whenever a memorial of any size is established, send an update to all contributors telling them how the funds were (or will be) used.

✓ Do a feature story on some of the memorial gifts you have received in past years and how those gifts impact those you serve.

✓ Create a recognition wall or walkway or some other lasting tribute to anyone who has been memorialized at your charity.

✓ Hold a yearly memorial service inviting the family and friends of those who have been memorialized in the past.

The most effective way of promoting memorial gifts is by showing the public how grateful you are to be named the recipient of a memorial.

2 Host an Annual Memorial Service

If your organization is the type that encourages memorial gifts and you want to draw more attention to that form of giving — and encourage people to add to memorial funds — consider hosting an annual memorial service at your facility.

An annual memorial service might include the following elements:

❑ Inviting the family and friends of all who have been memorialized as a result of gifts to your charity.

❑ Establishing an ongoing committee or advisory group to oversee changes and improvements to your program.

❑ Including an honor roll of everyone who has been memorialized that is included in your printed program.

❑ Having some sort of permanent display that lists the names of those who have been memorialized.

❑ Having someone make remarks about how the legacy of these deceased individuals will live on through the mission and work of your organization.

❑ Reading the names of those who have been memorialized at some point during your service.

❑ Inviting those in attendance to consider adding to named memorial funds.

Any sort of memorial service or reception serves to honor those whose family and friends connected with your cause.

3 Timing and Tact are Key To Establishing Named Memorials

Don't underestimate the importance of exploring major gift opportunities — or at least planting the seed — during the loss of a loved one.

Although it's important to use a great deal of tact in determining if and when you should broach the subject of a memorial with the deceased's loved ones, it is very appropriate to at least outline options when family members come to you or publicly announce that memorial gifts may be directed to your charity.

When that does occur, follow these guidelines:

1. **Cover procedures for handling memorial gifts as soon as you are notified.** Explain that all memorial gifts directed to your charity will be placed in a holding account until you and the appropriate family member(s) can meet to determine how they will be used. Also inform the family that, in addition to sending donors a note of thanks, the names, addresses and gift amounts will be shared with the family.

2. **Be sure your charity is well represented at the funeral and/or wake.** If your charity has been or may be named a recipient of memorial gifts, it's only appropriate that your presence is obvious. You may even want to provide flowers or a plant.

3. **Follow up within days.** Depending on circumstances and loved ones' wishes, set an appointment to meet and review memorial possibilities. Have a standard presentation developed — such as the example at right — to outline gift possibilities.

Timing and tact are key in determining when and how to approach the family of the deceased.

Prepare Memorial Gift Options to Share

- **If memorial gifts amount to less than $1,000:** Have a prepared wish list of needs — perhaps identified by your development or memorial committee — with attached dollar amounts. Include a range of dollar amounts and uses. This allows families to decide on the exact use of memorial funds without simply having funds "disappear" into your organization's general budget. Explain that the memorial — plus names of all who contributed — will be listed in your organization's annual report of contributors.

- **For memorial gifts totaling between $1,000 and $10,000:** Once again, share a wish list of needs, only this time identify more significant needs that include "naming opportunities" based on the overall amount contributed toward the memorial. Memorial gifts totaling $2,000, for instance, could be used to name an item — a flowing water fountain or a meeting room table — while a gift of $9,000 might name an office or a particular room in honor of someone.

- **For memorial gifts that may amount to $10,000 or more:** Gifts totaling $10,000 or more — even if pledged by family members over a period of years (or through a bequest) — could be used to establish various types of named endowment funds or to name even more significant capital projects (e.g., The Ned Otto Cancer Center, The Leo & Loretta Block Reading Room). Once again, it's helpful to have an identified list of gift opportunities. With this level of giving, however, it's important that the donor have some say in shaping the exact use of the gift to develop a greater sense of ownership in the project.

---

4 ### One Easy Way to Make Weddings Work for You

Today, planning a wedding often goes beyond choosing the venue, color schemes and flowers to choosing a worthy charity to celebrate on the big day as well.

What do you do when a couple calls to say they would like to use their wedding as a way to support your cause? Are you prepared to offer opportunities for their guests to do so?

If you don't have any formal programs set up to make weddings work for you, suggest that the bride and groom do an old-fashioned dollar dance, with the money going to benefit your organization instead of the bride and groom.

5 ### Tribute Gift Form Facilitates Donations

Tribute gifts are a meaningful way to honor loved ones or celebrate important anniversaries. They are also a great way to acknowledge the life's work of retired educators, says Julie Krause, executive director of the Appleton Education Foundation (Appleton, WI).

Krause estimates that the foundation receives some 50 tribute gifts a year, but the number varies widely. "If an educator who was well known and liked passes away, we can receive quite a few donations in a short period of time."

Tribute donations are facilitated by the tribute gift form pictured at right. The form — developed by a retired educator serving on a foundation committees — aims to collect all necessary information while alerting the donor to the possibility of employer matching programs.

The key to leveraging tribute gifts, says Krause, is consistency of publicity to the right audience, namely retired staff members, parents, alumni and long-time supporters.

Source: Julie Krause, Executive Director, Appleton Education Foundation, Appleton, WI. Phone (920) 832-1517. E-mail: jkrause@cffoxvalley.org

Tribute gifts can serve to honor the legacy of long-time employees.

Content not available in this edition

6 Acknowledge Memorials Timely and Appropriately

When someone informs you that they wish to have your charity become the recipient of memorial contributions, how do you handle such gifts? Do you have a system in place?

Here are some procedures you may want to implement as a part of your memorials acknowledgment process:

- When a memorial gift is received, send a message of appreciation to the donor within 48 hours.

- Inform the donor that the deceased's family will be notified of their thoughtful gesture.

- If possible, inform the donor how the memorial gift will be used by your charity.

- Depending on the number of memorial gifts being received and over what period of time, regularly provide the deceased's family with a written account of who has made memorial contributions. Include addresses and gift amounts so the family can also acknowledge gifts if they so choose.

- When you produce an annual list of contributors, include a list of memorials established during the fiscal year along with a list of those who contributed to each memorial.

Your response to memorial gifts will impact those that may follow. Have a system in place for promptly acknowledging memorial gifts.

7 Take Memorial Gifts a Step Further

Many nonprofits gladly accept memorial gifts, but that's often where the relationship ends — with a onetime gift. The sole opportunity that presented itself to establish a relationship with all those who made a contribution ends as soon as it began. Depending on the number of memorial gifts your charity receives, there could be a number of opportunities to establish a relationship with those who make a contribution in memory of someone.

To build a relationship with memorial contributors, take these actions:

1. Have a sound gift acknowledgment procedure in place. In addition to thanking each contributor in a personal way, provide to the deceased's family the list of contributors, along with amounts and addresses.

2. Be sure to add all names to your mailing list.

3. List the names of the deceased (in bold) in your annual roll of contributors along with the names of each who contributed to their memory.

4. Host a memorial service once a year at your facility — inviting all those who made memorial contributions — to remember those who died that year. Use the occasion to cultivate relationships with those who attend and provide tours of your facilities.

5. Produce a memorial book that is displayed and contains the names and dates of all who have been memorialized at your organization.

6. For memorial gifts that collectively amount to a sizeable sum, meet with the family to discuss ways in which the funds might be used, including the establishment of a named endowed fund that the family could add to over time.

Acceptance of memorial gifts should involve a series of follow up steps completed in a timely manner.

8 Leave No Questions Unanswered In Memorial Donors' Minds

What gift acknowledgment procedures do you follow when someone makes a memorial gift to your charity?

In addition to informing the family of the deceased of memorial gifts — who gave, when and how much — be sure to inform the contributor that the family of the deceased will be notified of the gift.

The example shown here helps clarify the charity's intent to inform the family of the deceased.

Dear <Name>:

We want to take this opportunity to thank you for your recent gift in memory of <name of deceased>. We know <name of deceased>'s family will want to know of your thoughtful gesture, so we will inform them within the next few days.

In addition, when our 2011 Annual Honor Roll of Contributors is distributed in <month>, your name will appear as a memorial contributor under the name of <name of deceased>.

---

9 Pending Option Gives Grieving Donors Time

When a loved one dies, families can become overwhelmed with all of the arrangements, decisions and grief.

Bonny Kellermann, director of memorial gifts, MIT (Cambridge, MA), says giving families time to consider all of their options ensures a meaningful gift to the school.

"Very often, when a family has lost a loved one, they are not ready to decide the details of how to memorialize them," Kellermann says. "Allowing a cushion of time to make this decision is greatly appreciated by the families."

"Often, when a family has lost a loved one, they are not ready to decide the details of how to memorialize them. Allowing a cushion of time to make this decision is greatly appreciated."

MIT allows families to establish funds with a purpose to be determined later through their pending memorial gift accounts. The decision of what to use the funds for can be deferred for up to two years. When the account is established, families are informed that any funds not designated within two years will be used for unrestricted purposes.

The pending option gives families time to think about an appropriate, meaningful memorial and allows time for them to receive memorial gifts from other people, which can be a factor in determining how the fund will be used.

Donors also benefit emotionally from the pending option.

"Many families really appreciate the fact that they can postpone this decision to a time after they have grieved or dealt with estate issues," says Kellermann. "The donor benefits by not being forced to make a decision at a time that is very stressful."

As a result, MIT also benefits. "Since the donors have the opportunity to take time to consider what is really important to them," Kellerman says, "they may be inclined to give more than they might have otherwise given."

Source: Bonny Kellermann, Director of Memorial Gifts, MIT, Cambridge, MA. Phone (617) 253-9722. E-mail: bonnyk@MIT.EDU

Patience and empathy are key when there's a death involved. Memorial decisions should never be rushed.

10

Tribute Program Recognizes Caregivers, Raises $1 Million

Putting a creative twist on tribute gifts, a California healthcare system has raised more than $1 million in less than four years.

Through the Guardian Angel Tribute Program for Sharp HealthCare (San Diego, CA), a patient can honor a special caregiver by making a donation in his or her name. There is no minimum donation, and patients can honor individuals or entire departments.

"This is a way for our patients to recognize any of their caregivers — a nurse, a physician, a housekeeper — who has done something wonderful for them," says Christina Jordan, senior development officer.

Here's how the tribute program works:

- Patients in a Sharp HealthCare's hospital receive a bookmark introducing the tribute program. The bookmark, left when housekeeping staff clean a room, features the program's logo, brief description and place to write special caregivers' names.

- Four to six months after the patient's hospital stay, he or she receives a direct-mail piece that further explains the Guardian Angel program and invites patients to honor a physician, nurse or other caregiver with a donation in his or her name. Additionally, tabletop displays with donation envelopes are at each of the nurses' stations, as well as some offices.

- When gifts arrive, development staff send a thank-you to the donor within 48 hours.

- Anyone named as a guardian angel receives a letter and special lapel pin. For a person's first recognition, the patient relations director presents the letter and takes a photo of the recipient, sharing details of the patient's story when provided. Since it is common for caregivers to receive recognition multiple times (one doctor has 81 pins), those receiving pins two through nine and 11 or more are simply sent a letter and pin. The 10th recognition earns a gold pin.

- The development staff mails the donor a second thank-you letter with a photo of the caregiver receiving his or her pin. Jordan notes that the picture taken at the initial presentation is used each time that person is honored.

- Early in the calendar year, donors receive a direct mail piece inviting them to submit a second donation in honor of their guardian angel to celebrate National Doctor's Day in March. As a gift for the physicians, the development office compiles a Doctor's Day booklet that lists guardian angels and donors who honored them.

Since implementing the tribute program four years ago, Jordan says, they have given out more than 5,300 pins to 1,577 guardian angels, with gifts in honor of the recipients exceeding $1 million. The average gift is $250 and the largest, $300,000.

Jordan credits the success of the program — which grew out of a similar, smaller-scale program in place at one of the organization's hospitals — to its simplicity and its natural fit with the The Sharp Experience, a system-wide initiative which focuses on making Sharp HealthCare the best place to work, practice medicine and receive care.

"The biggest benefit is connecting and establishing the relationship among the donor, physician and foundation," she says. "It connects those three dots."

Source: Christina Jordan, Senior Development Officer, Sharp HealthCare, San Diego, CA. Phone (858) 499-4811. E-mail: christina.jordan@sharp.com

Who says tribute programs are only good for nickel-and-dime gifts?

11   Memorial Giving Tips

Whenever your agency receives memorial gifts in remembrance of a recently deceased individual, be sure to point out endowment fund gifts to the family of the deceased should they choose to add to what has been given thus far — making the memorial even more permanent.

12   Tribute Tree Program Roots College in Its Past

With environmentally conscious moves taking center stage, now is the perfect time to launch a tree-planting campaign to benefit your nonprofit.

Hastings College (Hastings, NE) has a long tradition of tree planting beginning with the first spring planting season in 1883, says Matt Fong, director of alumni development. Through a new Tribute Tree program, Fong says, friends of the college can help that tradition continue.

The program began when fundraising efforts were wrapping up for the college's new science building. Fong says, "We were looking for ways to build the greenscape and let people continue giving." Here's how the program works:

For a $500 gift, the donor has a tree planted in his name, or the name of anyone he chooses.

Donors make a $500 donation to the program. In return, the college plants a tree of the donor's choice, selected from a predetermined list, and orders a plaque for the tree, which includes the type of tree and the name of the person being honored or memorialized. The donor's name and a tribute quote can be included on the plaque. Donors are encouraged to attend the tree-planting ceremony and bring family members with them.

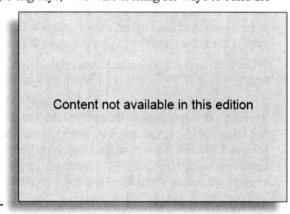

Content not available in this edition

To ensure success in the planting and growing process, the college's physical plant department works with a dedicated Professor Emeritus and the state Arboretum to determine which trees will thrive in the Nebraska climate. In addition, all trees that are planted are somewhat more mature trees, ranging six to nine feet in height. If, even with all these safeguards, the tree fails to thrive, Fong says the college will replace it if necessary, "though we may make a different suggestion about the type of tree or the location if it doesn't work after a few attempts."

The majority of the funds raised go to the college's Arboretum account so the greenspace can be maintained.

While only 10 to 20 trees have been purchased so far, the program is generating much interest, Fong says, especially after the college's recent tree-planting re-enactment. Even without that though, Fong says he expects the program to catch on. "Campuses are beautiful, natural settings. People are interested in things that beautify the campus and live on for a long time."

Source: Matt Fong, Director of Alumni Development, Hastings College, Hastings, NE. Phone (402) 461-7786. E-mail: mfong@hastings.edu

13   Share Your List of Memorial Gift Opportunities

If you want people to consider your organization for memorial gifts, develop a wide-ranging wish list of memorial gift opportunities to draw from when those times arise.

Turn to your memorial gifts committee to help identify gift opportunities. Develop a simple memorial gift opportunities brochure to share with families and distribute to appropriate locations: churches, synagogues and funeral homes. You may also wish to include the brochure (or the list) in other mailings to make your constituency aware of those memorial opportunities.

What might your memorial gifts brochure include? Consider these possibilities:

- A brief description of your organization's mission and services.
- A list of memorial gift opportunities that includes brief descriptions and costs.
- A list of memorials received during the past fiscal year.
- A statement of how memorials will be recognized.
- A panel that the recipient can fill out, detach and return with a memorial gift.
- Contact information for anyone wishing to explore a memorial gift.

Be sure to include a wide range of gift amounts and opportunities, and review the list as often as quarterly to remove items that have been selected and address new needs.

Charge your memorial gifts committee with responsibility for identifying appropriate memorial gift opportunities.

14   Benches Offer Beautiful and Comfortable Memorial

"When our campus looks good, we look good," says Maria Clark, administrative assistant for advancement, Oklahoma Christian University (Oklahoma City, OK).

That simple truth is a major motivator for the university's memorial bench program. Building community is another inspiration for the effort, says Clark.

"It was a natural initiative in our effort to make our campus more attractive, comfortable and student- and visitor-friendly," she says.

The pledge for each bench is $1,500, which covers the cost of the bench, a bronze plaque to memorialize or honor someone of the donor's choosing, and helps fund a maintenance endowment specifically for the bench program.

Clark says the endowment is important because maintenance has proven to be one of the most challenging parts of the program.

"Our benches are made of teakwood and need to be treated twice a year. We are currently looking at switching to a new bench to help lower the number of man hours needed to keep the benches in top shape. The benches are important to many people and we want them to look their best all year long."

Another important consideration is planning where the benches will go, she adds.

To date, 70 benches have been pledged and nine more are waiting to be placed across campus.

Source: Maria Clark, Administrative Assistant for Advancement, Oklahoma Christian University, Oklahoma City, OK. Phone (405) 425-5094. E-mail: maria.clark@oc.edu

Often times memorial gifts require sufficient financial support to endow the future maintenance of whatever is being funded.

15 Do Pet Memorials Make Sense For Your Organization?

Pet memorials: Humane societies do it. And with the ever-increasing popularity of pets and growing number of people who consider their pets as important members of their families, even some other types of nonprofit organizations are beginning to do it.

Could your organization justify inviting memorial gifts in memory of a beloved pet?

If you can start with a few individuals who choose to do this, publicize their acts of love in your honor roll of contributors and elsewhere to encourage others to do the same. Over time, you may be pleasantly surprised by the number of people who are drawn to make a contribution in memory (or in honor) of their pets.

Increasing types of nonprofit organizations are beginnnig to encourage pet memorials.

16 Encourage the Living By Remembering the Deceased

Show the living how the memory of deceased benefactors — those who have remembered your charity through their estates — is being kept alive.

Your ongoing acts of stewardship for those no longer living will serve to encourage others to make planned gifts as well.

Ways to pay tribute to deceased benefactors may include:

- Names on buildings, offices, engraved brick walkways/walls.
- Names on endowed funds or ongoing programs.
- Names associated with annual awards: Notable friends/donors, annual stipends to outstanding employees or those served by your agency and more.
- Feature articles in your publications that point out the deceased's legacy to your charity and those you serve.
- An annual listing of all (the deceased included) planned gift donors.
- An annual memorial service recognizing deceased benefactors.

17 Follow Up With Those Who Make Memorial Gifts

What sorts of follow up do you take with those who make memorial (even in tribute) gifts to your nonprofit? They obviously receive some sort of thank you from your organization, but what else occurs?

Whenever you receive a sufficient number and/or amount of memorial gifts to do something significant — start a scholarship, purchase a major piece of equipment or renovate or refurbish a room — everyone who helped make that project possible should be updated on its progress and included in celebrating its completion.

Those follow-up actions may include but not be limited to: a tour or demonstration, receiving a photo of the completed project, being invited to an unveiling or dedication, having their names listed in your honor roll of contributors and more.

As memorial donors witness your thoughtful acts of stewardship, they will become more likely to remember your organization in other ways as well.

Be sure to update everyone who helped make particular memorial gift projects possible.

18 Memorial Flowers Shower Hospice With Additional Revenue

If April showers bring May flowers, what do three-dimensional paper flowers in a Garden of Memories bring? The annual memorial tribute at Angela Hospice (Livonia, MI) has brought $43,000 to the organization, along with joy and comfort to the families of the 1,446 people who have been memorialized in the past two years.

Held each May, Garden of Memories invites the hospice's constituents to submit the names of loved ones they would like to honor. Those names are embossed on paper leaves and added to a display in the Care Center lobby that includes three-dimensional paper flowers, the embossed leaves and a booklet that records each honoree's name. Events Coordinator Barb Iovan says they also sometimes offer to print another leaf, which people can take home with them.

Donations are optional, says Iovan, but most choose to donate, with the average being around $35 per tribute.

The Garden of Memories is on display for the month of May and has brought a very positive response.

Iovan says, "The first year the response was so overwhelming we had to add an additional section to the display to allow for more flowers and leaves! In our second year, we added two more large displays."

Proceeds benefit the free-of-cost programs for hospice patients and their families, including special programs for children and teens as well as loss of spouse and loss from suicide.

Source: Barb Iovan, Events Coordinator, Angela Hospice, Livonia, MI. Phone (734) 953-6045. E-mail: biovan@angelahospice.net. Website: www.angelahospice.org/events/

Make a point to remember the memory of loved ones in lasting ways.

Content not available in this edition

Content not available in this edition

The above mailer invites supporters and constituents of Angela Hospice to take part in the Garden of Memories fundraiser.

19   Memorial Fund Options Help Focus Donor Intent

When Nancy Cushing-Daniels — beloved Spanish professor at Gettysburg College (Gettysburg, PA) — passed away in June 2009, her family approached college officials with an idea for a memorial fund. Their idea: to honor Cushing-Daniels' memory and passion for both learning languages and embracing cultures around the world.

If only it was always so easy to determine and honor donor intent.

It can be, if you have options, says Ashlyn Sowell, interim vice president for development, alumni and parent relations.

"We try to be prepared (for inquiries into memorial options) by having options," says Sowell. "For example, we have some benches and trees on campus that we designate for families who want a physical memorial. For other folks, we discuss funds like Professor Cushing-Daniels', which is more specific and restricted."

Sowell says college officials do not do a great deal of active fundraising for memorial gifts, letting the families drive that for the most part. What is most important, says Sowell, is being patient and understanding. "Memorial funds take time," she says, "and there are many emotions involved."

Source: Ashlyn Sowell, Interim Vice President for Development, Alumni and Parent Relations, Gettysburg College, Gettysburg, PA. Phone (717) 337-6503.
E-mail: asowell@gettysburg.edu

Whether it's in print form or not, it's wise to have plenty of memorial gift options in mind.

20   Don't Let Memorial Donors Fall Through the Cracks

What happens to the name of someone who makes a onetime memorial gift to your organization — someone with no previous ties to you? Is the name automatically added to your mailing list? Are any future attempts made to contact the onetime donor?

Far too many nonprofits willingly accept memorial gifts but fail to follow up in establishing a relationship with those who make first-time gifts.

Have a plan of action for those who make first-time gifts to your institution or agency by following up methodically. In addition to adding them to your mailing list:

1. Include a personalized thank you note or letter that makes mention of the person being memorialized, pointing out his/her relationship to your organization and why he/she was proud of being associated with you.

2. Within 60 days of the gift, send another letter (along with a brochure) that recalls the donor's memorial gift and makes the case for you meeting with him/her to share more of what your organization is all about. State at the conclusion of your letter that you will phone within the next few days to set an appointment. (If the donor's place of residence makes it impossible for you to meet face-to-face, make a phone call to reiterate your appreciation and chat about what your organization is doing.)

3. Include a "memorial and in tribute gifts" section in your annual report and list all donors under the names of those "in tribute" or "in memory of" individuals.

4. Send an anniversary letter that points out the donor's thoughtful memorial gift made one year prior and invites the donor to contribute again this year. Offer the option of making another gift in memory of the deceased individual.

Don't let one-time memorial or in-tribute donors fall through the cracks.

21

Revamped Tribute and Memorial Program Lets Donors Target Gifts

The Detroit Institute of Art (Detroit, MI), a cultural mainstay in Michigan for 125 years, has grown to one of the largest, most significant collections in the United States, comprising a multicultural survey of human creativity from prehistoric through the 21st century.

Growing right along with it is the museum's revamped Tribute and Memorial Program. Since the new program was launched in 2009, they have served over five hundred donors. This is a 47 percent increase in the number of gifts since the new program started.

Annual Fund Officer Jessica Stephens says clearly the new program has been met with enthusiasm. So what about the new program has made the most difference? The recently enhanced program offers donors the opportunity to highlight one of four key areas of the museum's mission. Recipients receive a tasteful acknowledgment featuring one of the museum's iconic works of art. Donors receive a thank you note and tax receipt for full deductibility.

Stephens explains the four key areas for giving below:

- **"Heritage"** gifts of $20 or more help ensure the museum remains open to the public and the art supporters have come to love and appreciate will be available for future generations. The cover of the acknowledgment card features Vincent van Gogh's, Portrait of Postman Roulin.

- **"Educator"** gifts of $75 or more support vital education initiatives at the DIA, ensuring that people young and old can continue the lifelong process of learning about art. The acknowledgment card features The Window by Henri Matisse.

- **"Protector"** gifts of $200 or more help support the conservation and preservation of each work of art in the DIA's permanent collection, ensuring its importance and value are never diminished. The acknowledgement features Albert Joseph Moore's, Study for Birds.

- **"Scholar"** gifts of $500 or more help support scholarship, ensuring that the DIA's curators and art educators are able to conduct research on the museum's collection and develop themes for exhibitions and catalogues. The cover of the card contains a picture from the DIA's collection Rachel Ruysch, Flowers in a Glass Vase.

Having these options available for donors has personalized the program and made a big difference. "Donors appreciate the ability to personalize the message, the ease of making a gift and the ability to choose a specific need in the museum's operational budget to support," says Stephens.

Source: Jessica F. Stephens, CFRE, Annual Fund Officer, Detroit Institute of Arts, Detroit, MI. Phone (313) 833-6760. E-mail: jstephens@dia.org.

Would you like to see memorial gifts climb by as much as 50 percent? See what the Detroit Institute of Art did to make that happen.

22 ### Memorial to Young Leader Inspires Emerging Leaders

The founding members of the Skip Cline Young Leadership Society of Morton Plant Mease Foundation (Clearwater, FL) recognized a desire of younger adults in the community to become more involved with their hospitals. They also recognized a natural connection in naming the society after their friend, Harry Sykes "Skip" Cline, Jr., who died an untimely death.

To the society's founders, "Skip embodied the ideals of a young leader," says Eric Barsema, community impact manager. "Skip was also raised in a family who contributed time, treasure and talent to our community and to Morton Plant Hospital.... They thought the group could build on his family's tradition of community involvement and philanthropy."

The society has raised more than $360,000 since being founded in 2004.

Members, aged 21 to 45, commit to make gifts of at least $500 annually. Members also commit to becoming better informed and more involved with their hospitals through a variety of social and educational events, including happy hours, fundraising events and educational lectures, as well as opportunities to mingle with physicians and hospital leadership. Generally, there is some type of event for members every month.

Donations are typically unrestricted, going to the hospital's area of greatest need. Barsema says the society is leaning toward designating gifts to specific projects in the hospital, a request the foundation is more than happy to accommodate.

With approximately 250 members, the group's size does pose a bit of a challenge, Barsema says: "Many of the founding members were in their late 30s when they launched the society, and now, five years later, are asking to be able to stay a part of the group after they turn 46."

The society's retention rate of more than 90 percent speaks to Barsema's unique dilemma, though he admits it's not a bad one to have. "Of all the foundation's annual giving societies," he says, "Skip Cline members seem to have the greatest camaraderie and pride for their philanthropic support of the hospitals of Morton Plant Mease."

Source: Eric Barsema, Community Impact Manager, Morton Plant Mease Foundation, Clearwater, FL. Phone (727) 462-7036. E-mail: mpmfoundation@baycare.org

Formalize your memorial giving program by giving it a name that holds special significance for your organization.

23 ### Five Ways to Promote Your Brick Campaign

Engraved brick campaigns are a great way to raise money for a specific project or program while beautifying an outdoor area. They also make great ways to encourage both memorial and in-tribute gifts.

Here are five ways to promote your brick campaign:

1. Include the campaign brochure in gift acknowledgments to donors who give to your annual fund or other programs.

2. Create a website specifically for promoting the brick campaign. Include information about where the money raised will go, how to purchase a brick, criteria for wording on the bricks, a map of where the bricks will be located, etc.

3. Send an e-mail solicitation to constituents for whom you have e-mail addresses, directing them to the brick campaign website for more information or to purchase a brick.

4. Create a traveling display for your brick campaign for external events, speaking engagements, etc.

5. Place ads about the campaign in your organization's newsletter, special donor publications and magazine.

24 'Buy A Brick' Covers Many Types of Projects

Start a "buy a brick" program that invites memorial and in-tribute giving. Here are six projects that the buy-a-brick concept has been used to fund:

1. **A wall.** Massillon Public Library (Massillon, OH) is selling bricks for installation in a new wall beside the library's new entrance. Website: www.massillon.lib.oh.us/construction/buy-a-brick.htm

2. **An entrance pathway.** The Children's Museum at Saratoga (Saratoga Springs, NY) is selling bricks for a new brick pathway leading to the museum's entrance. Website: https://w257.securedweb.net/cmssny/www/buyabrick.html

3. **A courtyard.** Icarus International, Inc. (Kitty Hawk, NC) is selling bricks for a commemorative courtyard for its Monument to a Century of Flight project. Website: www.icarusinternational.com/buy-a-brick.html

4. **A patio.** Hudson Valley Community College (Troy, NY) is selling bricks to build a "President's Patio," a brick patio located outside one of the college's buildings. Website: www.hvcc.edu/50/brick.html

5. **An amphitheater.** Bricks will be laid in the Hershey Foods Amphi-theater (Hershey, PA) of the new Children's Garden at Hershey Gardens. Website: www.hersheygardens.org/childgarden/buyabrick.htm

6. **A plaza.** The Naval Training Center Foundation (San Diego, CA), is selling bricks to create three Legacy Plazas within its new Promenade Center. Website: www.promenadecentre.org/news-2004-06-27.php

For many donors, seeing someone's name permanently displayed adds more meaning to their memorial or in-tribute gift.

Create a Virtual Brick Memorial Layout

The Houston Golf Association placed a virtual layout of the brick memorial for their Golfers Against Cancer program on their website (**www.golfersagainstcancer.org/chip200d.html**). A directory that accompanies the numbered layout lists donors by name alphabetically with their brick number beside their name.

"We do a lot of sales through mail and have out-of-state donors," says Rene Elliott, program manager of Golfers Against Cancer. "The virtual layout and directory shows these donors where their brick resides and how it looks."

Source: Rene Elliott, Program Manager, Houston Golf Association, Humble, TX. Phone (281) 454-7000. E-mail: relliott@hga.org

---

25 Secure a Challenge Gift Aimed at Memorial, In-tribute Giving

To encourage more people to think of your charity when it comes to memorials or in-tribute gifts, get someone to establish a challenge that will match anyone's memorial or in-tribute gifts up to a certain level.

If, for example, someone decides to make a $100 memorial or in-tribute gift to your charity in memory or in honor of someone, the challenger will also make a gift up to a certain level. So as a donor, I know that any memorial or in-tribute gift I make will receive an additional gift from the challenge donor.

Because of the uniqueness of this sort of challenge, it's sure to draw the attention of the public as long as it gets publicized sufficiently.

26 Giving Opportunities Start at $5,000 to Engage Donors

To involve people in the hospital's Imagine Campaign, officials with El Camino Hospital Foundation (Mountain View, CA) offer in-honor and memorial opportunities starting at $5,000.

Donors who wish to leave their philanthropic mark can give $5,000 for the organization's Nights at the Clinic program, $250,000 to name the laboratory, $1 million for an operating room, $3 million for the Oak Pavilion or up to $10 million to name the new main building.

To promote the opportunities, Lindsay Greensweig, director of major giving, says the foundation created folders to give to donors at one-on-one meetings, mail to prospective donors and distribute at VIP tours of the new hospital campus.

The folders include a campaign brochure that makes a compelling case for philanthropy by detailing highlights of the new hospital campus; the quarterly campaign newsletter; brochures for hospital programs supported by the foundation; and the list of the honor and memorial opportunities.

To date, donors have made 10 honor and memorial gifts totaling $5 million.

The two-phase campaign is all-inclusive, focusing on the hospital program and bricks and mortar. The first phase, finished a year early, brought in $25 million in four years and focused on gaining philanthropic support for new programs.

The second phase, launched in September 2008, aims to raise another $25 million in three to five years to coincide with the hospital's golden anniversary. This campaign will focus more on the honor and memorial opportunities, while raising money for hospital programs.

The campaign is scheduled to conclude in 2013.

Source: Lindsay Greensweig, Director of Major Giving, El Camino Hospital Foundation, Mountain View, CA.
Phone (650) 988-7849.
E-mail: Lindsay_Greensweig@elcamino-hospital.org

Develop a handout that's specific to memorial and in-honor-of giving. Use it during one-on-one meetings and in mailings to targeted groups.

Folders outlining giving opportunities to The Campaign for El Camino Hospital (Mountain View, CA) include flyers citing projects to fund at a wide range of major gift levels.

Content not available in this edition

27 Consider 'In Lieu Of' Gift Option

Persons who wish to support the Deborah Hospital Foundation (Browns Mills, NJ) have a unique way to do so: The In Lieu Of donation program. Ellen Krivchenia, director of national chapter services, explains:

How does the program work?

"People celebrating a special occasion such as a wedding, birthday or anniversary contact us to create personalized cards that either request guests donate to the hospital in lieu of purchasing a gift, or in the event of a wedding, the card might say that a donation has been made in the guests' names in lieu of them receiving party favors."

How do you make your program unique?

"My assistant handles the design aspect and works one-on-one with those making the requests to make sure they get exactly what they're looking for. From font to color palette, each one is unique."

Where/when do you promote the program?

"While we informally launched the program in 2008, we didn't promote it at all. But in January 2009, we started publicizing it on our website and through our print publication that goes out to our foundation members. Since then, we have had about 10 new clients with whom we've worked."

What is the average donation?

"We're averaging about $500 per event. I think as more people see our cards at events, the more interest we'll get and I anticipate donations will increase over time."

Who is taking advantage of this program?

"Individuals who are looking for more meaningful ways to spend their money. If a bride and groom can make a donation to the hospital rather than buy bags of mints for their reception tables, they'll do it. It's the same with the couple celebrating their 50th wedding anniversary — they don't need anything, why not encourage guests to make a donation that can help save a life instead?"

Source: Ellen Krivchenia, Director of National Chapter Services, Deborah Hospital Foundation, Browns Mills, NJ. Phone (669)893-3372. E-mail: dhfnjro@deborahfoundation.org Website: www.deborahfoundation.org

Follow this example and create personalized cards your constituents can use for events (weddings, birthdays, anniversaries), requesting their guests to donate to your cause rather than bringing a personal gift.

28 Be Creative When Looking for Naming Opportunities

When Legion Arts, a Cedar Rapids, IA-based art center, was damaged by flood water in 2008, officials knew renovation would be expensive. And because selling naming rights would be key to paying the $7 million bill, they got creative.

In addition to traditional naming opportunities, the organization gave donors and supporters the opportunity to purchase the right to name one of six urinals or 15 toilets in the newly redesigned facility. Each $1,000 gift was recognized with an engraved plaque, and committed donors were offered a private tour of all facilities to pick the fixture of their choice.

"Here's your chance to honor a loved one, a colleague, a favorite artist or yourself," proclaimed an e-mail sent to center supporters, announcing the opportunity. "You could join with your neighbors to salute a beloved legislator or council representative. Express your respect for a teacher or mentor. Or go in together with a couple of co-workers to surprise your boss. The possibilities are endless."

Clearly this approach would not work for every organization or campaign. But it is an undeniable fact that humorous, tongue-in-cheek fundraising efforts can be every bit as successful as more sober ones, and they certainly make more of an impression. The Legion Arts opportunity, for example, made the pages of newspapers throughout the Midwest and beyond.

29 · Garden Naming Options Offer Fertile Ground for Future Growth

When marking a milestone, create opportunities for named gifts that engage major donors up front and provide options for ongoing stewardship.

In 2005, Hospice and Palliative Care of Greensboro (HPCG) celebrated its 25th year of service to the community. And though the organization did not have capital needs at that time, officials were concerned about proactively growing their endowment, says Paul Russ, vice president of marketing and development. So they conducted a fundraising campaign focused on endowment, raising more than $3 million and establishing 13 new named endowment funds.

With no "bricks and mortar" associated with the campaign, officials needed another way to offer naming opportunities to major donors, Russ says. So they created a 25th Anniversary Garden that commemorated the anniversary and honored the leadership of volunteers and donors who helped secure HPCG's future through endowment giving.

The garden, which fills a formerly vacant cement slab outside of the hospice's main building, features an archway covered with a sculpture of wrought metal vines and leaves. Donors who made pledges of $25,000 and above were listed on the sculpture wall (see giving levels, below).

"Thematically, we felt that endowment gifts are like seeds that reach fertile ground, growing over time to provide nourishment and comfort," says Russ. "The 25th Anniversary Campaign helped create a sound financial foundation from which the agency can continue to grow."

Hospice officials worked with a local architect and local provider of donor recognition programs, Metal Décor (Greensboro, NC), to design the archway and metal sculpture. Costs included $35,000 for redesign of the front entrance and $17,000 for the leaf-themed donor recognition system. Officials included an artist's rendering of the archway and description of the project in solicitation packets for the 25th Anniversary Campaign.

Visitors, including donors, frequently comment on the project, he says. "They appreciate that it visually represents how endowments work. Donors also appreciate the naming opportunity, even though traditional bricks and mortar were not part of the project."

In fact, says Russ, because the project was so well-received, officials duplicated the vine system on the reverse side of the archway. The second set of vines honors anyone who establishes a planned gift for HPCG.

Source: Paul Russ, CFRE, Vice-President of Marketing and Development, Hospice and Palliative Care of Greensboro, Greensboro, NC. Phone (336) 478-2502. E-mail: pruss@hospicegso.org

This excerpt shows garden-themed giving levels offered to donors to the 25th Anniversary Garden of the Hospice and Palliative Care of Greensboro (Greensboro, NC).

Content not available in this edition

30 ### Include Tribute, Memorial Gift Options On Pledge Forms

If you would like to increase the number of memorial and/or in-tribute gifts your charity receives each year, be sure all pledge forms include that gift option along with other gift options.

In addition to specifying the name of the individual being honored or memorialized, the donor can instruct the development office to notify appropriate individuals of the gift. Portions of two pledge forms are shown below.

Don't overlook including memorial and in-tribute giving options on all of your pledge cards.

Tribute and Memorial Gifts

❏ This gift is in memory of _____
and/or
❏ This gift is in honor of _____

A notification of your tribute or memorial gift will be sent to the individual listed below. The gift amount will not be indicated.

Individual to receive notification _____

Address _____

City _____ State _____ ZIP _____

Name _____

Occasion (Optional) _____

Occasion (Optional) _____

City State ZIP

Your gift will be acknowledged in accordance with your instructions, and the gift amount will not be disclosed.

City State ZIP

Daytime Phone

E-mail Address

31 ## Added Language Can Aid in Memorial Gifts

Adding some simple language to your e-mail's automated out-of-office reply ensures that your organization can provide details on memorial gifts even when you are out.

Bonny Kellermann, director of memorial gifts, MIT (Cambridge, MA), includes the following in her auto-reply specifically to assist persons needing it for obituaries:

Here's a simple idea worth doing!

> "If you are looking for information to include in an obituary regarding memorial gifts, you can refer to the following language: 'In lieu of flowers, gifts may be made to MIT for the [name of fund]. Checks should be payable to MIT and mailed to Bonny Kellermann, Director of Memorial Gifts; 600 Memorial Drive, W98-500; Cambridge, MA 02139. Please include a note stating that your gift is in memory of [name].' You can also reference the following webpage for additional information about memorial gifts: http://giving.mit.edu/ways/memoriam/."

Use similar language on your phone message and website to provide important information in a timely manner to families considering including memorial gift options in honor of a loved one who has passed away.

Source: Bonny Kellermann, Director of Memorial Gifts, MIT, Cambridge, MA. Phone (617) 253-9722. E-mail: bonnyk@MIT.EDU

Look for distinctive ways to honor those who have or had a connection to your organization.

 32 **Butterflies in Garden Honor Lives, Raise Awareness**

The staff at Hospice and Palliative Care of Greensboro (Greensboro, NC) was looking for a way to remember the children who had been a part of their Kids Path program and had died. Kids Path is a nationally recognized program that improves access to palliative home health and hospice services for medically fragile children and improves the capacity of children to cope with grief and loss related to medical issues.

During a staff retreat, they began brainstorming and settled on the idea of butterflies as a reminder of the playful nature of children. Sculptor Jim Gallucci was brought in and the rest, as they say, is history. Gallucci had recently seen a swarm of butterflies that led him to create colorful metal butterflies to honor the memories of the children.

Butterflies are added every three years as part of the Kids Path memorial service—one for each child that has died during the previous three-year time period. The cost varies depending on the number of butterflies needed, though very little maintenance is required once the butterflies are installed. Butterflies are located on a fence surrounding a garden behind the Kids Path building.

Program Director Marion Taylor says the memorials have been a very positive addition for the families they serve. "Families appreciate their child being remembered. Sometimes parents who have a child die are afraid people will forget that child. It's important to them to see the child's name and know their child is not forgotten." Taylor says some families even come to "visit" their child's butterfly.

Staff has also given positive feedback about it, since it gives them a way to memorialize the children too.

Source: Marion Taylor, Director, Kids Path Program, Hospice and Palliative Care of Greensboro, Greensboro, NC. Phone (336) 621-2500. E-mail: mtaylor@hospicegso.org.

33 **Acknowledge Volunteer Service with Memorial Gifts**

Have you considered honoring longtime volunteers after they've passed away?

At the Mississippi Valley Regional Blood Center (MVRBC) of Davenport, IA, volunteers who have passed are honored with a special gift to their family at the memorial service. A monetary gift to the person's memorial fund or a plant is sent to the family acknowledging the service of the volunteer.

Consider the following when instituting volunteer memorial gifts:

- Create a line item in your budget or a special fund that allows for acknowledgement of service by volunteers who have consistently served your organization over a designated period of years upon their passing. Parch reviewed internal documents and found that volunteers were included in the administrative policy of MVRBC up to $50 per memorial.

- Determine whether memorial gifts will be in monetary form to a memorial fund or a gift to the surviving members of the family.

- Add a personal note to the memorial card acknowledging that specific volunteer and their service such as, "Thank you for sharing your dad with us to serve our organization. The 15 years he served helped many people in need." Doing so will be especially meaningful to the volunteer's family.

Source: Kay Parch, Manager of Volunteer Relations, Mississippi Valley Regional Blood Center, Davenport, IA. Phone (563) 823-4112. Email: kparch@mvrbc.com. Website: www.bloodcenter.org

34 New Brochure Helps Create Interest In Tribute, Memorial Gifts

When the Detroit Institute of Art (Detroit, MI) decided to revamp their Tribute and Memorial Program in 2009, they decided to use familiar images to help promote the program. They also wanted to make the process as easy as possible for their donors.

Annual Fund Officer Jessica Stephens says the result is a program brochure designed to be warm and inviting, with works of art selected both for their familiarity to museum goers and for their emotional strength. A postage-paid self mailer makes it easier for donors to make a tribute or memorial gift, and personalize the message that will be sent to the recipient. Donors who prefer to use the DIA's website are met with the same ease in arranging a tribute or memorial.

Source: Jessica F. Stephens, CFRE, Annual Fund Officer, Detroit Institute of Arts, Detroit, MI. Phone (313) 833-6760. E-mail: jstephens@dia.org.

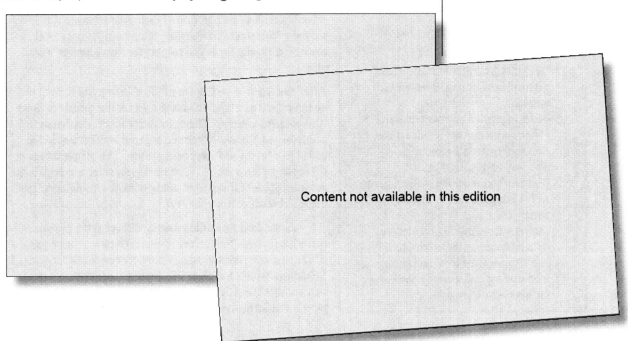

Content not available in this edition

35 Encourage the Living By Remembering the Deceased

Show the living how the memory of deceased benefactors — those who have remembered your charity through their estates — is being kept alive.

Your ongoing acts of stewardship for those no longer living will serve to encourage others to make planned gifts as well.

Ways to pay tribute to deceased benefactors may include:

- Names on buildings, offices, engraved brick walkways/walls.
- Names on endowed funds or ongoing programs.
- Names associated with annual awards: Notable friends/donors, annual stipends to outstanding employees or those served by your agency and more.
- Feature articles in your publications that point out the deceased's legacy to your charity and those you serve.
- An annual listing of all (the deceased included) planned gift donors.
- An annual memorial service recognizing deceased benefactors.

36 Honor Your Deceased Volunteers

When an active volunteer dies, those who worked closely with him/her experience a great loss. Long-time volunteers are very proud of their service. Members may find comfort and support by honoring the lost volunteer as a group. Here is how one volunteer organization does it:

Before the Service — When word of a volunteer's death reaches the board, the Compassionate Service chairperson contacts the family to offer assistance. A calling tree is used to inform members of the event. Funeral service plans, visiting times, chapel/mortuary address, and family wishes regarding flowers/donations are conveyed. If the family is displaying art, talents, photos or representations of life's interest, they usually include the volunteer's uniform. In this case, the chairperson arranges to have the uniform cleaned and recognition/service pins polished.

During the Service — Volunteers meet at a central location and travel to the service together. Wearing their uniforms offers immediate recognition of their connection to the deceased. Volunteers sit together, often occupying several rows, as a strong display of respect for the volunteer's service.

After the Service — Copies of the obituary and funeral program are posted in the volunteer area for the benefit of those who could not attend. The volunteer's name, death date, and total years/hours of service are engraved on a gold tag, added to a hardwood memorial plaque. The plaque hangs in the organization's lobby. The family receives a special letter advising them of this honor, along with disclosing donations made in behalf of the volunteer.

A standard for adding names was set at the organization's beginning. Volunteers who served two or more years or donated over one thousand hours of service are recognized. Volunteers whose health or life circumstances made it necessary for them to retire from service are not forgotten. If they meet the criteria, their names are added when they pass away.

Memorializing Volunteers

Volunteer memorials come in many forms. Need some examples?

- Designate a memorial wall space where photos of former volunteers can be added.
- Order imprinted bricks containing volunteer names and service dates. Add the bricks to a memorial walkway or garden spot.
- Donate a commemorative tree, along with a brass marker, in memory of the volunteer.
- During annual award ceremonies, remember volunteers with short vignettes on their lives and service, or with a photo and special mention on the back of the program.

---

37 Join Forces with Other Local Nonprofits

To draw more attention to the idea of memorial and in-tribute giving, join forces with your community's other nonprofit organizations to collectively evaluate what you might do together that encourages gifts of this nature.

Your collaborative efforts will draw more attention to memorial and in-tribute giving as a charitable option and may include some new fundraising strategies such as:

✓ Creating a brochure that lists all of your community's charitable organizations that can be placed in funeral homes and other appropriate venues.

✓ Placing a full-page ad in your community's newspaper that lists all charitable organizations and invites the public to consider memorial and/or in-tribute gifts to any or all of them. Depending on the size of your community, you might even want to list all memorials received by all organizations during the previous year as a way to recognize those individuals.

38 Reach Out to Families With a Children's Wall

Capital campaigns are always in need of creative funding strategies, particularly at middling levels of donation. Approaches that generate ongoing relationships (as opposed to just one-time gifts) are similarly sought-after. Reaching out to entire families, including young children, accomplishes both goals at once.

Officials at the Kauffman Center for the Performing Arts (Kansas City, MO) established just this kind of outreach with their Children's Wall, a donor recognition project that allows children, grandchildren or other young friends of donors to leave their handprint on a specially-designated section of the under-construction facility.

When completed, the project will feature 1,000 children's handprints arranged along the approach to the center's main lobby. Each entry will include the name of the child being honored and the year the handprint was created. (Hand prints can be captured and submitted remotely, ensuring appeal to supporters beyond the immediate Kansas City area.)

For $1,000 per handprint, donors can give a youngster special to them a one-of-a-kind experience, and center officials can begin building connections with a new generation of potential supporters — a win-win situation for all involved!

Source: Kauffman Center for the Performing Arts, Kansas City, MO. Phone (816) 994-7200. E-mail: contact@kauffmancenter.org.
Website: http://www.kauffmancenter.org/support/donate/childrens-wall

Here's a wonderful way to honor children who may have a connection to your organization.

39 Giving Tree Attracts Attention, Offers Lessons

Diane Pirollo, Vice President, Community Relations & Foundation Development, Jefferson University Hospitals, Methodist Hospital (Philadelphia, PA) says their Giving Tree, located in the hospital's lobby serves two purposes—recognizing donors at a giving level of $1,000 or higher and encouraging visitors to the hospital to give by putting giving front and center.

The tree, which has been in place since 2002, recognizes approximately 125 donors, and donations totaling over $550,000.

Each leaf is purchased at the $1,000 level. Increasing levels earn an acorn, acorn with cap, small and large stones and clouds.

In addition to the recognition factor, Pirollo says it is truly a beautiful centerpiece in the lobby. "It attracts attention and encourages gift-giving." Visitors are drawn to the display, which passively reminds them of the need for donations and the recognition afforded those who give.

Pirollo does have one suggestion though, for those looking to implement a similar recognition piece—make sure you include long-range considerations in your planning. "We are an urban community hospital in a working class neighborhood, which is becoming increasingly diverse. Gifts of less than $1,000 are not currently displayed, which makes it difficult for community members to memorialize loved ones. $1,000 is pricey for our demographic area. I wish I had started at the $500 level."

Source: Diane Pirollo, Vice President, Community Relations & Foundation Development, Jefferson University Hospitals, Methodist Hospital, Philadelphia, PA.
Phone (215) 952-9006. E-mail: Diane.Pirollo@jeffersonhospital.org.
Website: www.jeffersonhospital.org

40 Brick Program Helps to Pave the Way

As the three little pigs learned, a brick can provide a solid foundation. That dependability is also why many schools use brick programs to raise money.

Rather than copy traditional brick programs that generally include brick engravings on a structure in a specific location, the Detroit Public Schools Foundation (Detroit, MI) took a unique approach.

"Our brick program offers donors the opportunity to actually have a piece of the school's history in their possession by ordering an engraved, personalized brick that they can display in their home or office," says Regina Fortushniak, development officer of the Detroit Public Schools Foundation.

At Cass Technical High School (Detroit, MI), organizers of its brick program launched the effort Dec. 1, 2010, in conjunction with the first-ever annual appeal. To date, the program has raised about $4,000. "Our plan is to do a more comprehensive launch this spring, engaging the community and notable Cass Tech alumni and sharing the stories of existing brick contributors who are very pleased with their brick," Fortushniak says.

The program provides Cass Technical High School alumni, friends, family and educators the opportunity to purchase a brick from the former Cass Tech building with proceeds going to benefit students at the new high school. "They provide the opportunity for donors to not only give to a cause they care about, but to also hold onto a piece of that cause," she says. "It adds a more personal touch to giving, more than a general donor acknowledgment can."

Donors may choose from one of three bricks:

- Bronze: This brick features a bronze plate bearing the school's name and a picture of the school for $57.60.

- Silver: Mounted on a walnut base, this brick holds a silver plate that can be personalized with an alumni's name and graduation year for $87.60.

- Gold: This brick that comes with a cherry acrylic base in a Lucite encasement with a gold plate that can also be personalized for $148.40.

"We've been pleasantly surprised that our biggest seller has actually been our most expensive piece, the gold brick," Fortushniak says.

The Cass Tech commemorative brick program is the first in a series of four brick campaigns. Soon the foundation will launch programs for three additional high schools. Proceeds from these campaigns will also benefit Detroit Public Schools students.

Members of the Detroit Public Schools Foundation use social media including a Facebook page and Twitter to share information about their brick campaigns. They also send out e-newsletters and promote the program in local print, radio and television media outlets.

Source: Regina Fortushniak, Development Officer, Detroit Public Schools Foundation, Detroit, MI. Phone (313) 873-3414. Email: rfortushniak@detroitpsfoundation.org Website: www.detroitpsfoundation.org

---

Successful Brick Programs

Brick by brick, schools are building needed funds through sales of bricks that can be personalized and installed on school property.

The Nicolet High School Foundation (Glendale, WI) has offered a brick program since 1999 to raise money for a teen center at the school. To date, nearly 200 bricks have been sold, most to parents of students, followed by alumni.

To reach different pricing levels, the effort offers three different pricing levels:

- $60 for a 4-x-8-inch individual brick
- $250 for an 8-x-16-inch family/group brick
- $1,000 for a 16-x-16-inch corporate brick

A professional brochure is used to get the word out about the brick program, along with information provided through large mailings to current parents, alumni and some businesses; parent newsletters and other communications with the parent body; by personally approaching area businesses with information on the corporate bricks; and through back-to-school nights and parent-teacher conferences.

Orders are taken during the school year and the bricks are installed he following summer.

At Millard South High School (Omaha, NE), the Brick by Brick Program began in 2004 as a fundraiser for the schools Hall of Fame banquet. The banquet recognizes teachers, alumni, students and community members who play a significant role in the success of the school.

For $100, a brick can be purchased and displayed in the school's courtyard. Each brick usually contains a name, the named person's connection to the school, and dates of significance. This fundraiser runs year round and is publicized through alumni e-mails, the Millard Foundation and school newsletters.

School officials say they have sold several hundred bricks since 2004.

Sources: Tracy Hancock, Office of the Registrar, Millard South High School, Omaha, NE. Phone (402) 715-8262 Email: THancock@mpsomaha.org
Christine Macon, Executive Director, Nicolet High School Foundation, Nicolet High School, Glendale, WI. Phone (414) 351-7561.
Email: chris_macon@nicolet.k12.wi.us

---

41 Six Tips for Handling Memorial Donations

When a loved one dies, the family often suggests a nonprofit organization for people to send donations to in lieu of flowers.

Bonnie McCullough, executive director of the New York State Funeral Directors Association (Albany, NY), shares tips to make the donation process easier for the nonprofit, the funeral director and, most importantly, the grieving family:

1. Have a program that's flexible. Each funeral director may handle relationships with nonprofits differently.

2. Remember that philanthropy is an important part of the culture, particularly during a time of grief for a family, but not a mandate.

3. Ask the funeral home staff if they will list your organization's contact information on their website. Many of them will.

4. Contact the funeral home to give a contact name and phone number for your organization once a family includes a charity in an obituary. Families will often call the nonprofit for a listing of those who have contributed so they can send thank you's.

5. Understand that the funeral director's unpredictable schedule may require him/her to call you back at another time.

6. Consider sending a single rose or simple thank-you card to the family for naming your particular nonprofit in an obituary. McCullough says, "The kind gesture will pay dividends."

Source: Bonnie McCullough, Executive Director, New York State Funeral Directors Association, Albany, NY. Phone (518) 452-8230. E-mail: info@nysfda.org. Website: www.nysfda.org

Your procedures for handling memorial gifts should be all-inclusive, taking into consideration the family of the deceased, your organization and even the funeral director.

42 Good for the Donor, Good for You

Giving a gift in honor of a person feels good to the donor, and a tribute or memorial gift that goes into your general operating fund is especially good for your organization. That's according to Kelly Ptacek, senior director of sustaining gifts for Creighton University (Omaha, NE).

"Operational funds are the most flexible for the organization, where money can be used for the greatest need. In our case, the university is able to say 'our number one objective this year is scholarships for students because of the recession and the financial pinch that families are feeling,' and we can make scholarship dollars available from the unrestricted general operating pot," Ptacek says. But she adds that it's also more difficult to raise money for operations than it is for a special project. "That's why tribute gifts that are not earmarked are so important."

Ptacek suggests encouraging tribute gifts by providing information about them on your website with links in e-mails and newsletters that can easily connect the prospective donor to the tribute gifts section. "There they can learn how to go about giving a gift, and why it's a wonderful thing for the organization," she says.

Source: Kelly Ptacek, Senior Director of Sustaining Gifts, Creighton University, Omaha, NE. Phone (402) 280-1485. E-mail: kellyptacek@creighton.edu. Website: www.creighton.edu

Provide information about memorial and in-tribute giving on your website, and include links in emails and newsletters that can connect donors to these website pages.

Memorial Tributes Help Save Lives

"If you had the chance to save the life of someone you love, wouldn't you take it?" That is the question asked of visitors to the philanthropy portion of The Scripps Research Institute (La Jolla, CA) website. "Your generosity can impact the future of medical history." And they are hoping that people will do that with one of their newest philanthropic tools, the Scripps Research Tribute.

The research tributes, which were started a few years ago with the assistance of Sankynet (www.sankynet.com) in New York, NY, began as a way to bring a more personal approach to funding for biomedical research, says Scripps Research's Philanthropy Associate Elliot Wolf. Individuals can create a tribute either in honor or in memory of someone special in their life, by uploading a photo, writing a personal note and choosing a designation for all gifts made to that tribute. "For example," says Wolf, "If I were to create a tribute in memory of a grandparent who had Alzheimer's, I could choose that all gifts made to that tribute be directed to Alzheimer's research."

A unique URL is given to each tribute and whomever visits their tribute page can leave a comment or make a donation. The page can also be forwarded to their friends, family and colleagues to make gifts to the tribute.

Wolf says even without any real advertising or marketing to speak of, there have already been about 30 tributes set up, raising anywhere between $10 and $10,000, depending on how the tribute creator shares it with friends and family.

Wolf says the tributes are a great way to engage a memorial-tribute donor and also gives them a tool to reach out to their friends. "Biomedical research can seem so cold and academic. This is a way to make it warm and personal, while honoring the legacy of a loved one through research that may one day result in cures. It also allows people to have an outlet for simply sharing comments, as well as making gifts."

Wolf says they are just starting to market the tributes, with several marketing efforts in the works right now, and are excited to see how much traction they get moving forward.

Source: Elliot Wolf, Philanthropy Associate - Marketing & Donor Research, The Scripps Research Institute, La Jolla, CA. Phone (858) 784-2721. E-mail: elliotw@scripps.edu. Website: https://www.scripps.edu/tribute/home/

Approach the Deceased's Former Employer

In some instances, it may be appropriate to approach the deceased's former employer with an invitation to support an existing memorial that's been started at your organization. Although an employer has no obligation to support a memorial, your willingness to make a personal call and extend an invitation is most appropriate and may in fact be appreciated.

The former employer may be willing to extend an invitation to all employees to support the memorial and, in some cases, an employer may even put the invitation to employees in the form of a matching gift: "The company will match any memorials gifts made by employees."

The personal visit also allows you to share a written news brief — making mention of the memorial through your organization — that may be used in the company's internal newsletter. In addition to the announcement, the news brief can include a brief description of the deceased's connection to your organization along with contact information.

45 Annual Arbor Day Ceremony
Serves as Gentle Reminder

Events Coordinator Barb Iovan, Angela Hospice (Livonia, MI) says their annual Arbor Day ceremony serves as a gentle reminder that, "because there is no timeline for grieving, we are still here and available for grief support, whether one utilized Angela Hospice for the care of their loved one or not."

Individuals who have experienced a loss during the previous year, and have donated money for a memorial tree, bench, stone or brick to be placed on the hospice's beautifully landscaped grounds are invited to attend the Arbor Day celebration with as many friends and family as they would like. Many bereavement staff provide support as well.

When checking in, guests receive a packet which includes a photo of their tree, brick, bench or stone. The event begins with a brief program held outside, under a portico, adjacent to a fountain.

Following the program, volunteers accompany guests, particularly those who arrive alone, to where their memorial item is placed. Each tree has a ribbon corresponding with the ribbon on the photograph in the guest's packet.

Guests take the opportunity to have photos taken at the site and engage in a heartfelt moment — entire families often attend. Following the viewing of their item, participants are invited to a light catered lunch.

Iovan says guests appreciate the opportunity to be with friends and family, and in some cases reunite with the bereavement staff member who has been helpful to them during a very challenging time of their lives. They also like that they have a place to come and honor their loved one in a serene setting. "Family members do come back to visit their memorial on occasion and are welcome to do so at their leisure."

Source: Barb Iovan, Events Coordinator, Angela Hospice, Livonia, MI. Phone (734) 953-6045. E-mail: biovan@angelahospice.net. Website: http://www.angelahospice.org/events/

46 Invite In-tribute Gifts
Honoring 'Employee of the Month'

Does your organization have any sort of program in place that honors your employees, such as an "employee of the month" program?

Take your employee recognition program to the next level: Invite the employee's friends, family and associates to make an in-tribute gift in honor of the individual.

Let's say you have an "employee of the month" program in place. Once an employee has been named, ask that individual to select from a list of funding projects that he/she would like to get funded at your organization. It doesn't have to be an expensive item but something that's near-and-dear to the heart of that employee — a classroom/learning tool for the teacher; a useful resource for a nurse who's been named employee of the month. Then sit down with that employee and develop a list of his/her contacts, people to whom you can announce his/her selection as "employee of the month" and then extend an invitation for them to help fund that project in his/her honor.

By adding this funding feature to the employee recognition, you are: a) adding a new level of recognition to your employee of the month program, b) funding a needed project and c) getting people to support your cause who might otherwise contribute nothing.

Evaluate all of your organization's recognition programs to see if this concept might be appropriate for any of them as well.

47   Online Tribute Pages Help Raise Further Funds

"If you had the chance to save the life of someone you love, wouldn't you take it?"

That is the question asked on the philanthropy portion of The Scripps Research Institute (La Jolla, CA) website, and officials there are hoping that people will answer it with one of their newest philanthropic tools, the Scripps Research Tribute.

The research tributes, which were started a few years ago with the assistance of Sankynet (www.sankynet.com) in New York, NY, began as a way to bring a more personal approach to funding for biomedical research, says Scripps Research's Philanthropy Associate Elliot Wolf.

Individuals can create a tribute either in honor or in memory of someone special in their life, by uploading a photo, writing a personal note and choosing a designation for all gifts made to that tribute. "For example," says Wolf, "If I were to create a tribute in memory of a grandparent who had Alzheimer's, I could choose that all gifts made to that tribute be directed to Alzheimer's research."

A unique URL is given to each tribute and visitors to the page can leave a comment or donation. The page can also be forwarded to their friends, family and colleagues to make gifts to the tribute.

Wolf says even without any real advertising or marketing to speak of, there have already been about 30 tributes set up, raising anywhere between $10 and $10,000, depending on how the tribute creator shares it with friends and family.

Wolf says the tributes are a great way to engage a memorial-tribute donor and also gives them a tool to reach out to their friends.

"Biomedical research can seem so cold and academic. This is a way to make it warm and personal, while honoring the legacy of a loved one through research that may one day result in cures. It also allows people to have an outlet for simply sharing comments, as well as making gifts."

Wolf says they are just starting to market the tributes, with several marketing efforts in the works right now, and are excited to see how much response they get moving forward.

Source: Elliot Wolf, Philanthropy Associate – Marketing & Donor Research, The Scripps Research Institute, La Jolla, CA. Phone (858) 784-2721. E-mail: elliotw@scripps.edu. Website: https://www.scripps.edu/tribute/home/

 48   Before Your Fiscal Year Ends....

Looking for ways to generate some additional gift revenue as your fiscal year comes to an end? Try this:

During the last month of your fiscal year, distribute a list of all memorials and in-tribute gifts that have been realized to date. Include the name of the person being memorialized or honored along with the names of those who have given in recognition of those individuals.

Include a statement that reads, "The following list of individuals have been recognized with memorial and in-tribute gifts during the current fiscal year which will conclude on.... We invite you to make a gift remembering or honoring any of those persons listed here. If we receive your gift on or before [date], your name will be added to this list of donors which will be reprinted and distributed in our Annual Honor Roll of Donors to be distributed next [date]. Show your respect to anyone listed here — or anyone not shown here — by making your memorial or in-tribute gift today."

49 Guardian Angel Program Offers Tangible Way to Say Thanks

Is your health-related organization looking for a way to help patients show appreciation for the care they received? If so, a guardian angel program might be just what the doctor ordered.

Such programs, in which patients give a donation in honor of a staff member who made a difference in their stay, might seem simple, yet they offer multiple advantages. Jen Miller, annual gifts officer at Friends of St. John's Hospital (Springfield, IL), describes four reasons her organization started a program:

- "One reason was because patients who are grateful for their care ask what they can do, and the Guardian Angel program gives them an easy way to say 'thank you.'"

- "Second, it recognizes staff members who give outstanding care. This is a very popular part of the program. Guardian angels are recognized by the hospital administration, their managers and their peers."

- "Third, it raises awareness of the Friends of St. John's, and is a way to keep us in the mind of staff members. We try to remind managers and staff to connect us with patients who want to do something to give back, and it becomes meaningful when they can do that in the form of a gift."

- "Fourth, obviously, we did it to raise money."

How does the program work? Miller explains that when the foundation receives a guardian angel gift, a "pinning ceremony" is scheduled for the employee, his or her co-workers and supervisory administrators. Many of the angels are nurses, but all staff members, from doctors to housekeeping staff, are eligible.

At the ceremony, the staff member receives a special lapel pin that is worn on a uniform or nametag, which lets everyone know he or she was named a guardian angel. Any note of thanks that accompanied the gift is read aloud, and once a year the names of all guardian angels are included in the hospital's donor newsletter.

In its first two years, the program has elicited over 150 gifts, with an average amount of almost $50 each — the recommended amount is $25. But just as importantly, it has reinforced the hospital's mission and values. Miller notes that even the program's challenges are positive: "We are just starting to come across employees receiving multiple nominations, and we are working with the pin company to produce second- and third-honor bars that can be added to the pin itself. It's a great problem to have."

Adds Miller, "Patients are thankful for the opportunity to acknowledge the person that made a difference to them during their stay, employees are happy for being acknowledged for a job well done, managers can identify staff members that are continually providing exemplary care, and the hospital has more resources to fund patient programs."

Sources: Jen Miller, Annual Gifts Officer, Friends of St. John's Hospital, Springfield, IL. E-mail: Jen.Miller@St-Johns.org

Give patients a way to show appreciation for the care they received by honoring one or more of your employees or volunteers.

50 **Thank-a-Teacher Cultivates Annual Fund Stewardship**

The form letters and mass mailings of annual fund giving often lack the personal engagement that comes with major gifts. Wanting annual fund donors to experience a greater sense of stewardship, the Education Annual Fund at the Stanford University School of Education (Stanford, CA) launched its Thank-a-Teacher campaign.

Donors were encouraged to make that year's gift in honor of a favorite teacher — from Stanford, elementary school or any level in between — and write a letter saying why that particular teacher was so important to them. In return, the dean of the School of Education would send a personal note to that teacher as well.

"My hope was to encourage more people to feel connected to their giving, and to build in a stewardship component for the regular annual fund donors."

"My hope was to encourage more people to feel connected to their giving, and to build in a stewardship component for the regular annual fund donors," explains Lisa Rying, associate director of the Stanford Fund for Undergraduate Education. "I wanted to allow annual giving donors to have that sense of connection, in the way that most major gift donors enjoy."

The Thank-a-Teacher campaign drove home the importance of the School of Education's mission. "I did teach for a couple of years, so I knew from having been a teacher that it meant the world, getting a nice, little note saying, 'Thank you, you inspired me.' I figured, why can't we do that for the greater School of Education population?" says Rying.

Very little needed to be added or altered in the existing annual fund collateral to launch the Thank-a-Teacher campaign. And on the back end, Rying's only extra duty was to write and print the thank-you notes which the dean then signed.

The positive outcomes from the Thank-a-Teacher campaign were different than what Rying anticipated. For example, it did not affect the level of giving, rate of participation, size of gift or likelihood that somebody would give a gift, she says. The reason? "It essentially gave people homework," she says, explaining that donors might need to track down contact information for former teachers, as well as write a letter explaining why they chose to honor a particular teacher.

However, an upside was that "It made many people read the appeal, and they're still giving in response to that appeal several months down the road," says Rying. Another valuable result has been the number of stories, shared through donors' letters, that the Education Annual Fund has used as positive website content.

"Overall, even though the dollars or numbers didn't go up, we did see it as a successful appeal," says Rying. "It was, and is, hard to find ways to steward regular annual fund donors, so in that way, the dean loved it."

Source: Lisa Rying, Associate Director, The Stanford Fund for Undergraduate Education, Arrillaga Alumni Center, Stanford, CA. E-mail: lrying@stanford.edu

51 Ideas for Increasing Memorial & In-tribute Gift Support

51 **Search Your Budget to Identify Funding Possibilities**

Do you have a readily available list of funding opportunities that exists for donors who wish to make memorial or in-tribute gifts? If so, how extensive is it?

You may be surprised by the number and range of gift opportunities that exists within and even outside of your organization's yearly operations budget.

To be sure no gift opportunities are being overlooked, take the time to go through your nonprofit's budget line by line to weigh each item's potential as a memorial or in-tribute gift opportunity. Consider big-ticket and inexpensive items equally as you develop an extensive wish list. Don't be hesitant about listing even those items that you consider more questionable. You can always review and prioritize your list after a thorough review.

After reviewing your operations budget in its entirety, think about needs outside of your budget that have never received a high enough priority to be included. Survey your employees to get their input on unfunded needs, then add those items to your list.

Once you have compiled what you consider to be a complete list of funding opportunities, revisit each item to weigh its attractiveness as an item that merits being on your list of memorial and in-tribute gift opportunities. In addition to deleting some items from your list, you may choose to categorize funding opportunities in various ways (e.g. by gift type, gift amount).

Once you have that list, decide how to make the best use of it. You may choose to post it on your website or develop a handout that can be selectively shared with would-be donors, or you may choose to do a feature article in your magazine that talks about memorial and in-tribute gifts and includes your list as an illustration.

Creating your list from scratch is the hard part. Once you have a list, it can be reviewed and evaluated on a yearly basis to decide on what items should be added or deleted.

Make a point to review your organization's operations budget on a yearly basis to identify funding opportunities worthy of memorial or in-tribute gifts.

Analyze Your Budget for Memorial, In-tribute Gift Opportunities

You may be surprised by the number of memorial and in-tribute gift opportunities you find by analyzing each line item of your nonprofit's budget.

Here's a very small sampling of possible funding opportunities you may come across:

Outdoor —
- Walkways
- Gardens
- Fountain
- Driveways
- Lighting
- Seating
- Patio

Buildings —
- Offices
- Rooms
- Lobbies
- Dining areas
- Labs
- Meeting rooms
- Study rooms
- Seating
- Auditorium

Equipment —
- Labs
- Computers
- Surgical
- Vehicles
- Exercise equipment
- Wheelchairs

Miscelleous —
- Books
- Decorative items
- Car seats
- Ceremonial items
- Dishes
- Clocks
- Furniture
- Lighting
- Sound system